LAUGHTER

THE BEST
MEDICINE

JOKES FOR EVERYONE

Vincenzo Berghella

Copyright page

Copyright Year: 2007

ISBN No.   978-0-6151-7920-9

From the same author:

- **Ridere, la migliore medicina. Barzellette per bambini.** www.lulu.com or www.amazon.com (2007) [Italian]

- **Obstetric Evidence Based Guidelines. Informa Healthcare, London, UK, and New York, USA (2007)** www.jefferson.edu/mfm or www.amazon.com [English]

- **Maternal-Fetal Evidence Based Guidelines. Informa Healthcare, London, UK, and New York, USA (2007)** www.jefferson.edu/mfm or www.amazon.com [English]

Index

To my relatives and my friends, to see them laugh

Introduction

Why this book? Life is already too serious an affair to be taken seriously. I've been a doctor for over 20 years, and deal with life and death decisions on a daily basis. I just finished publishing two medical texts, on the topics I deal with, obstetrics and maternal-fetal medicine. I hope, and believe, that these two large 'heavy' texts will help improve the health of mothers and babies worldwide. Now I feel the need to 'take a break', switch gear. I believe this book of jokes will also improve health, in fact directly improve the wellbeing of you readers, without intermediaries. Laughter increases secretion of catecholamines and of endorphins, increases oxygen in blood, relaxes arteries and so decreases blood pressure, and also increases the immune response.[1] These jokes have been collected from private emails I received directly from friends in the last 10 years. I believe, and science proves it, that laughter is a wonderful medicine. It's important, no matter the circumstances, to keep some of our youth innocence. You do not quit playing because you become old; you become old because you quit playing.[2] Since I do not know how to tell jokes 'live', I've written them down for you in these books: in English, and in Italian (different ones), since I've spent my first 20 years of my life in Italy and the last 24 in my new home, the US. I'm far from ashamed: to look a fool is the secret of a wise man.[3] In fact I hope to get even closer in spirit to you, since it's said that laughter is the shortest distance between two people. If you have comments, or jokes to add, my email is vincenzo.berghella@jefferson.edu. This book is dedicated to all my true and care-free friends who have sent me jokes via email: Andres Aldrete, Stefano Bini, Biu Bruijn, Sean Daly, James and Olivier de Givenchy, Tony Johnson, Andy Klinghoffer, Don Korkis, Scott Mulder, Nabil Moukarzel, Marco Pascali, Lucas Texeira, and their partners.

Enjoy!

Vincenzo Berghella

[1]Robin Williams, in 'Patch Adams'; [2]Oliver Wendell Holmes; [3]Edgar Allan Poe *(as seen on the wall of Café' Regio, in New York City)*

Quick ones

What does a bee sit on?
Its beeyond.

A person walks into a bar.
What does he says?
'Ouch'

How do you stop a rhino from charging?
You take his credit card.

Teacher: 'You missed school yesterday, didn't you?'
Pupil: 'Not a bit.'

Boss: 'You should have been here at 8 o'clock.'
Steno: 'Why, what happened?'

Weather prediction

The Indians asked their Chief in autumn, if the winter was going to be cold or not.
Not really knowing an answer, the chief replies that the winter was going to be
cold and that the members of the village were to collect wood to be prepared.
Being a good leader, he then went to the next phone booth and called the National
Weather Service and asked, "Is this winter to be cold?"
The man on the phone responded, "This winter was going to be quite cold indeed."
So the Chief went back to speed up his people to collect even more wood to be
prepared. A week later he called the National Weather Service again, "Is it going to
be a very cold winter?"
"Yes," the man replied, "it's going to be a very cold winter."
So the Chief goes back to his people and orders them to go and find every scrap of
wood they can find.
Two weeks later he calls the National Weather Service again: "Are you absolutely
sure, that the winter is going to be very cold?"
"Absolutely" the man replies, "the Indians are collecting wood like crazy."

Driving

Two elderly women were out driving in a large car, both barely large enough to see over the dashboard. As they cruised along, they came to an intersection. The stoplight was red but they just went on through.

The woman in the passenger seat thought to herself, "I must be losing it, I could have sworn we just went through a red light."

After a few more minutes, they came to another intersection, the light was red, and again they went right through. This time, the passenger was almost sure that the light had been red, but was also concerned that she might be seeing things. She was getting nervous and decided to pay very close attention.

At the next intersection, sure enough, the light was definitely red and they went right through it. She turned to the other woman and said, "Mildred! Did you know we just ran through three red lights in a row? You could have killed us."

Mildred turned to her and cried, "Oh shoot! Am I driving?"

Work

Why do I feel so tired?
For a couple of years I've been blaming it on lack of sleep and too
much pressure from my job, but now I've found out the real reason:
* The population of this country is 58 million.
* 24 million are retired.
* That leaves 34 million to do the work.
* There are 20 million at school, which leaves 14 million to do the work.
* Of this there are 7.5 million employed by the government, leaving
6.5 million to do the work.
* 2.7 million are in the armed forces, which leaves 3.8 million to do
the work.
* Take from the total the 3,770,000 people who work for Local
Authorities and that leaves 30,000 to do the work.
* At any given time there are 20,000 people in hospital, leaving 10,000 to do the
work.
* Now there are 9,998 people in prison.
* That leaves just two people to do the work.
* You and me.
And you're sitting at your computer reading jokes.

Self exam

According to statistics of Andersen Worldwide, around 90% of the professionals failed this exam. The questions are not that difficult. You just need to think.

1. How do you put a giraffe into a refrigerator?
The correct answer is:
Open the refrigerator, put in the giraffe and close the door.

The above question tested whether you are doing simple things in a complicated way.

2. How do you put an elephant into a refrigerator?
Wrong Answer:
Open the refrigerator, put in the elephant and close the refrigerator.
Correct Answer:
Open the refrigerator, take out of the giraffe, put it the elephant and close the door.

The above question tested your logic skills.

3. The Lion King is hosting an animal conference. All the animals attend except one. Which animal does not attend?
Correct Answer:
The Elephant! ...still in the refrigerator!

The above question tested your memory skills.

OK, if you did not answer the last three questions correctly, this one may be your last chance to testify your qualification to be a professional.

4. There is the river where the crocodiles live. How do you manage to cross it?
Correct Answer:
Simply swim through it. All the Crocodiles are attending the Animal Meeting!

The above question tested your comprehensive skills.

If you did not get any of the questions right, relax; you are perfectly qualified for a management position.

Courtroom exchanges

Actual quotes from the witness stand:

Q: What is your date of birth?
A: July fifteenth.
Q: What year?
A: Every year.

Q: What gear were you in at the moment of the impact?
A: Gucci sweats and Reeboks.

Q: This myasthenia gravis -- does it affect your memory at all?
A: Yes.
Q: And in what ways does it affect your memory?
A: I forget.
Q: You forget. Can you give us an example of something that you've forgotten?

Q: How old is your son, the one living with you?
A: Thirty-eight or thirty-five, I can't remember which.
Q: How long has he lived with you?
A: Forty-five years.

Q: What was the first thing your husband said to you when he woke that morning?
A: He said, "Where am I, Cathy?"
Q: And why did that upset you?
A: My name is Susan.

Q: And where was the location of the accident?
A: Approximately milepost 499.
Q: And where is milepost 499?
A: Probably between milepost 498 and 500.

Q: Sir, what is your IQ?
A: Well, I can see pretty well, I think.

Q: Did you blow your horn or anything?
A: After the accident?
Q: Before the accident.
A: Sure, I played for ten years. I even went to school for it.

Q: Trooper, when you stopped the defendant, were your red and blue lights flashing?
A: Yes.
Q: Did the defendant say anything when she got out of her car?
A: Yes, sir.
Q: What did she say?
A: What disco am I at?

Q: Is your appearance here this morning pursuant to a deposition notice which I sent to your attorney?
A: No, this is how I dress when I go to work.

REMEMBER - A PERSON WITH A LAW DEGREE ASKED THE QUESTIONS BELOW!!!
Q: Now doctor, isn't it true that when a person dies in his sleep, he doesn't know about it until the next morning?
Q: The youngest son, the twenty-year old, how old is he?
Q: Were you present when your picture was taken?
Q: Was it you or your younger brother who was killed in the war?
Q: How far apart were the vehicles at the time of the collision
Q: You were there until the time you left, is that true?
Q: How many times have you committed suicide?
Q: Are you qualified to give a urine sample?

HOW ABOUT THESE?
Q: So the date of conception (of the baby) was August 8th?
A: Yes.
Q: And what were you doing at that time?

Q: She had three children, right?
A: Yes.
Q: How many were boys?
A: None.
Q: Were there any girls?

Q: You say the stairs went down to the basement?
A: Yes.

Q: And these stairs, did they go up also?

Q: Mr. Slatery, you went on a rather elaborate honeymoon, didn't you?
A: I went to Europe, Sir.
Q: And you took your new wife?

Q: How was your first marriage terminated?
A: By death.
Q: And by whose death was it terminated?

Q: Can you describe the individual?
A: He was about medium height and had a beard.
Q: Was this a male, or a female?

Q: Doctor, how many autopsies have you performed on dead people?
A: All my autopsies are performed on dead people.

Q: All your responses must be oral, OK? What school did you go to?
A: Oral.

Q: Do you recall the time that you examined the body?
A: The autopsy started around 8:30 p.m.
Q: And Mr. Dennington was dead at the time?
A: No, he was sitting on the table wondering why I was doing an autopsy.

Q: Do you know if your daughter has ever been involved in voodoo or the occult?
A: We both do.
Q: Voodoo?
A: We do.
Q: You do?
A: Yes, voodoo.

Q: Now doctor, isn't it true that when a person dies in his sleep, he doesn't know about it until the next morning?

Q: The youngest son, the twenty-year-old, how old is he?

Q: Were you present when your picture was taken?

Q: Is your appearance here this morning pursuant to a deposition notice which I sent to your attorney?
A: No, this is how I dress when I go to work.

Q: All your responses must be oral, OK? What school did you go to?
A: Oral.

Q: Are you qualified to give a urine sample?

AND THE ALL TIME FAVORITE:

Q: Doctor, before you performed the autopsy, did you check for a pulse?
A: No.
Q: Did you check for blood pressure?
A: No.
Q: Did you check for breathing?
A: No.
Q: So, then it is possible that the patient was alive when you began the autopsy?
A: No.
Q: How can you be so sure, Doctor?
A: Because his brain was sitting on my desk in a jar.
Q: But could the patient have still been alive nevertheless?
A: It is possible that he could have been alive and practicing law somewhere.

Don't step on the ducks!

Three women die together in an accident and go to heaven. When they get there, St. Peter says, "We only have one rule here in heaven: don't step on the ducks!"
So they enter heaven, and sure enough, there are ducks all over the place.
It is almost impossible not to step on a duck, and although they try their best to avoid them, the first woman accidentally steps on one.
Along comes St. Peter with the ugliest man she ever saw. St. Peter chains them together and says, "Your punishment for stepping on a duck is to spend eternity chained to this ugly man!"
The next day, the second woman steps accidentally on a duck and along comes St. Peter, who doesn't miss a thing. With him is another extremely ugly man.
He chains them together with the same admonishment as for the first woman.
The third woman has observed all this and, not wanting to be chained for all eternity to an ugly man, is very, VERY careful where she steps.
She manages to go months without stepping on any ducks, but one day St. Peter comes up to her with the most handsome man she has ever laid eyes on... very tall, long eyelashes, muscular, and thin.
St. Peter chains them together without saying a word.
The happy woman says, "I wonder what I did to deserve being chained to you for all of eternity?"
The guy says, "I don't know about you, but I stepped on a duck!"

Bed Farts

An old man and his wife have gone to bed. After laying in bed for a few minutes the old man cuts a fart and says "seven points."
His wife rolls over and asks, "What in the world was that?"
The old man says, "Touchdown, I'm ahead 7 to nothing."
A few minutes later the wife lets one go and says, "Touchdown, tie score."
After about ten minutes the old man farts again and says, "Touchdown, I'm ahead 14 to 7."
Now starting to get into this the wife quickly farts again and says, "Touchdown, tie score."
The old man strains really hard but, to no avail. He can't fart, so not to be outdone by his wife, he gives it everything he has and strains real hard to get out just one more fart. Straining real hard the old man tries so hard he shits in the bed.
The wife asks, "Now what in the world was that?"
The old man replies, "Half-time, switch sides."

The World's First Blond Male Joke

An Irishman, a Mexican and a blond guy were doing construction work on scaffolding on the 20th floor of a building. They were eating lunch and the Irishman said, "Corned beef and cabbage! If I get corned beef and cabbage one more time for lunch I'm going to jump off this building."
The Mexican opened his lunch box and exclaimed, "Burritos again!
If I get burritos one more time I'm going to jump off, too."
The blond opened his lunch and said, "Bologna again. If I get a bologna sandwich one more time I'm jumping too."
Next day the Irishman opens his lunch box, sees corned beef and cabbage and jumps to his death.
The Mexican opens his lunch, sees a burrito and jumps too.
The blond opens his lunch, sees the bologna and jumps to his death also. At the funeral the Irishman's wife is weeping.
She says, "If I'd known how really tired he was of corned beef and cabbage I never would have given it to him again!"
The Mexican's wife also weeps and says, "I could have given him tacos or enchiladas! I didn't realize he hated burritos so much."
Everyone turned and stared at the blonde's wife. "Hey, don't look at me," she said. "He makes his own lunch."

Choking

One day, at a local buffet, a man suddenly called out: "My son's choking!
He swallowed a quarter! Help! Please, anyone! Help!"
A man from a nearby table stood up and announced that he was quite experienced at this sort of thing. He stepped over with almost no look of concern at all, wrapped his hands around the boy's gonads and squeezed. Out popped the quarter.
The man then went back to his table as though nothing had happened.
"Thank you!" the father cried. "Are you a paramedic?"
"No," replied the man. "I work for the IRS."

Slogans for women's tee-shirts:

1. So many men, so few who can afford me.
2. God made us sisters; Prozac made us friends.
3. If they don't have chocolate in heaven, I ain't going.
4. At my age, I've seen it all, done it all, heard it all ... I just can't remember it all.
5. My mother is a travel agent for guilt trips.
6. Princess, having had sufficient experience with prince, seeks frog.
7. Coffee, chocolate, men ... Some things are just better rich.
8. Don't treat me any differently than you would the Queen.
9. If you want breakfast in bed, sleep in the kitchen.
10. Dinner is ready when the smoke alarm goes off.
11. It's hard to be nostalgic when you can't remember anything.
12. I'm out of estrogen - and I have a gun.
13. Guys have feelings too. But like ... who cares?
14. Next mood swing: six minutes.
15. I hate everybody ... and you're next.
16. And your point is ... ?
17. If we are what we eat, I'm fast, cheap and easy.
18. Warning: I have an attitude and I know how to use it.
19. Of course I don't look busy ... I did it right the first time.
20. Do NOT start with me. You will NOT win.
21. You have the right to remain silent, so please SHUT UP.
22. All stressed out and no one to choke.
23. I'm one of those bad things that happen to good people.
24. How can I miss you if you won't go away?
25. Sorry if I looked interested. I'm not.

Dress

Mr. Clemens was vacationing on a riverboat casino on the Mississippi with his wife. By the second day, they were already fighting.
"Your dresses are too tight," he screamed. "You look like a tramp."
"Oh," she replied, "You want to see me in something long and flowing? If you find something long and flowing, let me know and I'll get in it."
So he pushed her into the river.

The Three Corporate Lessons:

Lesson Number One:
A crow was sitting on a tree, doing nothing all day. A small rabbit saw the crow, and asked him: "Can I also sit like you and do nothing all day long?"
The crow answered: "Sure, why not."
So, the rabbit sat on the ground below the crow, and rested.
All of a sudden, a fox appeared, jumped on the rabbit and ate it.
Moral of the story is:
To be sitting and doing nothing, you must be sitting very, very high up.

Lesson Number Two:
A turkey was chatting with a bull. "I would love to be able to get to the top of that tree," sighed the turkey, "but I haven't got the energy."
"Well, why don't you nibble on some of my droppings?" replied the bull. "They're packed with nutrients."
The turkey pecked at a lump of dung and found that it actually gave him enough strength to reach the first branch of the tree.
The next day, after eating some more dung, he reached the second branch.
Finally after a fortnight, there he was proudly perched at the top of the tree.
He was promptly spotted by a farmer, who shot the turkey out of the tree.
Moral of the story:
Bullshit might get you to the top, but it won't keep you there.

Lesson Number Three:
A little bird was flying south for the winter. It was so cold, the bird froze and fell to the ground in a large field. While it was lying there, a cow came by and dropped some dung on it. As the frozen bird lay there in the pile of cow dung, it began to realize how warm it was. The dung was actually thawing him out!
He lay there all warm and happy, and soon began to sing for joy.
A passing cat heard the bird singing and came to investigate.
Following the sound, the cat discovered the bird under the pile of cow dung, and promptly dug him out and ate him!
The morals of this story are:
1) Not everyone who drops shit on you is your enemy.
2) Not everyone who gets you out of shit is your friend.
3) And when you're in deep shit, keep your mouth shut.

Is Gas Too High?

You think a gallon of gasoline is expensive.
Diet Snapple 16oz for $1.29 equals $10.32 per gallon
Lipton Ice Tea 16oz for $1.19 equals $ 9.52 per gallon
Gatorade 20oz for $1.59 equals $ 10.17 per gallon
Ocean Spray 16oz for $1.25 equals $ 10.00 per gallon
Pint of milk 16oz for $1.59 equals $12.72 per gallon
STP Brake Fluid 12oz for $3.15 equals $ 33.60 per gallon
Vick's Nyquil 6oz for $8.35 equals $ 178.13 per gallon
Pepto Bismol 4oz for $3.85 equals $123.20 per gallon
Whiteout 7oz for $1.39 equals $25.42 per gallon
Scope 1.5oz for $0.99 equals $ 84.48 per gallon
And this is the REAL KICKER...
Evan water 9oz for $1.49 equals $ 21.19 per gallon
............$21.19 FOR WATER!!
You get the idea?? So next time you are at the pump, be glad your car
does not run on Nyquil, Scope, or Whiteout!

You know you've been **on-line too long** when...

You start introducing yourself as Jim at aol.com.
Your wife drapes a wig over the monitor to remind you of what she looks like.
You check your mail. It says "no new messages" so you check it again.
You name your children Eudora, Mozzilla, and Dotcom.
All of your friends have an @ in their names.
You tell the cab driver you live at http://123.elm.street/house/bluetrim.html
You tell the kids they can't use the computer because "Daddy/Mommy's got work
to do."
You get a tattoo that says "This body best viewed with Internet Explorer 5.0."
You ask the plumber how much it would cost to replace the chair in front of the
computer with a toilet.
You start tilting your head sideways whenever you smile. :-)
When your car crashes through the guardrail on a mountain road, your first instinct
is to search for the "back" button.

TGIF

A business man got on an elevator in a building. When he entered the elevator, there was a blonde already inside and she greeted him by saying "T-G-I-F". He smiled at her and replied "S-H-I-T". She looked at him, puzzled, and said "T-G-I-F" again. He acknowledged her remark again by answering "S-H-I-T". The blonde was trying to be friendly, so she smiled her biggest smile and said as sweetly as possible, "T-G-I-F" another time.

The man smiled back to her and once again replied with a quizzical expression, "S-H-I-T".

The blonde finally decided to explain things and this time she said "T-G-I-F........... T-hank G-oodness I-t's F-riday; get it?"

The man answered, "S-orry H-oney, I-t's T-hursday."

Speeding away

A senior citizen in Florida, who used to live in New York, bought a brand new Mercedes convertible. He took off down the road, flooring it to 80 mph and enjoying the wind blowing through what little hair he had left on his head.

This is great," he thought as he roared down I-95. He pushed the pedal to the metal even more. Then he looked in his rear view mirror and saw a highway patrol trooper behind him, blue & red lights blaring.

"I can get away from him with no problem" thought the man and he tromped it some more and flew down the road at over 100 mph. Then 110, 120 mph. Then he thought, "What am I doing? I'm too old for this sort of thing."

He pulled over to the side of the road and waited for the trooper to catch up to him. The trooper pulled in behind the Mercedes and walked up to the man.

"Sir," he said, looking at his watch. "My shift ends in 30 minutes and today is Friday. If you can give me a reason why you were speeding that I've never heard before, I'll let you go."

The man looked at the trooper and said, "Years ago my wife ran off with a Florida state trooper, and I thought you were bringing her back."

The trooper replied, "Sir, have a nice day."

Proofs

THREE PROOFS THAT JESUS WAS BLACK
1. He called everybody "brother"
2. He liked Gospel
3. He couldn't get a fair trial

THREE PROOFS THAT JESUS WAS MEXICAN
1. His first name was Jesus
2. He was bilingual
3. He was always being harassed by the authorities

THREE PROOFS THAT JESUS WAS JEWISH
1. He went into his father's business
2. He lived at home until he was 33
3. He was sure his Mother was a virgin, and his Mother was sure he was God

THREE PROOFS THAT JESUS WAS ITALIAN
1. He talked with his hands
2. He had wine with every meal
3. He worked in the building trades

THREE PROOFS THAT JESUS WAS A CALIFORNIAN
1. He never cut his hair
2. He walked around barefoot
3. He started a new religion

THREE PROOFS THAT JESUS WAS IRISH
1. He never got married
2. He was always telling stories
3. He loved green pastures

THREE PROOFS THAT JESUS WAS A WOMAN
1. He had to feed a crowd, at a moment's notice, when there was no food
2. He kept trying to get the message across to a bunch of men who just didn't get it
3. Even when he was dead, he had to get up because there was more work for her to do!

Pulled over

The car was pulled over by a highway patrolwoman for speeding.
As the officer was writing the ticket, she noticed several machetes in the car.
"What are those for?" she asked suspiciously.
"I'm a juggler," the man replied. "I use those in my act."
"Well, show me," the officer demanded.
The juggler took out the machetes and started juggling them; first three, then more until he was tossing seven at one time, overhand, underhand, behind the back, putting on a dazzling show in the breakdown lane and amazing the officer.
Just then, another car passed by. The driver did a double take, and said, "My God. I've got to give up drinking! Look at the test they're giving now."

Parachute

An airplane was about to crash, and there were 5 passengers left but only 4 parachutes.
The first passenger, George W. Bush said, "I am President of the United States and I have a great responsibility, being the leader of 300 million people, and a superpower, etc. I am also the smartest president ever." So he takes the first parachute, and jumps out of the plane.
The second passenger, said, "I'm Antoine Walker, one of the best NBA Basketball players, and the Boston Celtics need me, so I can't afford to die." So he takes the second parachute, and leaves the plane.
The third passenger, Hillary Clinton, said, "I am the wife of the former President of the United States, and a New York Senator, and I am the smartest woman in the world." So she takes the third parachute and exits the plane.
The fourth passenger, the Old Man, says to the fifth passenger, a 10-year old boy scout, "I am old and frail and I don't have many years left, so as Christian gesture and a good deed, I will sacrifice my life and let you have the last parachute.
The Boy Scout said, "It's OK, there's a parachute left for you. The world's smartest president took my backpack."

You Know You're Italian When...

1. You're 5'4", can bench press 325 pounds, shave twice a day and you still cry when your Mother yells at you.
2. Your Father owns 5 houses, has $300,000 in the bank and still drives a '76 Monte Carlo.
3. You share a bathroom with your 5 Brothers, have no money and drive a $45,000 Camaro or Firebird.
4. Your mechanic, plumber, electrician, accountant and travel agent are all blood relatives.
5. You consider dunking a cannoli in an espresso, a nutritious breakfast.
6. Your 2 best friends are your cousin and your brother-in-law's brother-in-law.
7. You are a card-carrying V.I.P at more than 3 strip clubs.
8. Despite the hair on your back, you still try to impress the ladies by wearing your "Just do me" tank top to the beach.
9. At least 5 of your cousins live on your street.
10. All 5 of those cousins are named after your Grandfather.
11. A high school diploma and 1 year of Nassau Community College, has earned you the title of "Professor" among your Aunts.
12. You are on a first name basis with at least 8 banquet hall owners.
13. If someone in your family grows beyond 5'6", it is presumed his mother had an affair.
14. There were more than 28 people in your bridal party.
15. You netted more than $50,000 on your first Communion.
16. At some point in your life, you were a D.J.
17. 30 years after immigrating, your parents still say: "Pronto" when answering the phone.
18. You have ever been in a fight defending Sly Stallone's thespian greatness.
19. Somewhere on your parents' property, there is a bathtub Madonna.
20. You build your house with 3 materials... brick, brick and wrought iron.
21. You have at least one sister that went to Beauty School.
22. Clothes from the Chess King will actually fit you.
23. It is impossible for you to talk with your hands in your pockets.
24. Have been to a funeral where talk of the deceased is: "He shoulda kept his big yap shut."

Bad times

"The woman's husband had been slipping in and out of a coma for several months, yet she had stayed by his bedside every single day.
One day, when he came to, he motioned for her to come nearer. As she sat by him, he whispered, eyes full of tears: "You know what? You have been with me all through the bad times. When I got fired, you were there to support me.
When my business failed, you were there. When I got shot, you were by my side. When we lost the house, you stayed right here. When my health started failing, you were still by my side. You know what?"
"What dear?" she gently asked, smiling as her heart began to fill with warmth.
"I think you're bad luck."

Dents

A nice looking blonde was driving and got caught in a really bad hailstorm.
Her cars was covered with dents, so the next day she took it to a repair shop.
The shop owner, seeing she was a blonde, decided he would have a little fun.
He told her just to go home and blow into the tailpipe really hard, and all the dents would pop out.
So the blonde goes home, gets down on her hands and knees and starts blowing into the tailpipe of her car.
Nothing happened. She blows a little harder and still nothing happens.
Just then, her roommate, another blonde, arrives home and sees what she is doing.
"What are you doing?" she asks.
The first blonde tells her how the repairman had instructed her to blow into the tailpipe in order to get all the dents to pop out. Her roommate, rolling her eyes, looks at her and says,........
"HELLO....you need to roll up the windows first!"

Al Gore

"If we don't succeed, we run the risk of failure."
"Democrats understand the importance of bondage between a mother and child."
"Welcome to Mrs. Gore, and my fellow astronauts."

"Mars is essentially in the same orbit...Mars is somewhat the same distance from the Sun, which is very important. We have seen pictures where there are canals, we believe, and water. If there is water, that means there is oxygen. If oxygen, that means we can breathe."

"The Holocaust was an obscene period in our nation's history. I mean in this century's history. But we all lived in this century. I didn't live in this century."

"I believe we are on an irreversible trend toward more freedom and democracy - but that could change."

"One word sums up probably the responsibility of any Governor, and that one word is 'to be prepared'."

"Verbosity leads to unclear, inarticulate things."

"I have made good judgments in the past. I have made good judgments in the future."

"The future will be better tomorrow."

"We're going to have the best educated American people in the world."

"People that are really very weird can get into sensitive positions and have a tremendous impact on history."

"I stand by all the misstatements that I've made."

"We have a firm commitment to NATO, we are a part of NATO. We have a firm commitment to Europe. We are a part of Europe."

"Public speaking is very easy."

"I am not part of the problem. I am a Democrat."

"A low voter turnout is an indication of fewer people going to the polls."

"When I have been asked who caused the riots and the killing in LA, my answer has been direct & simple: Who is to blame for the riots? The rioters are to blame. Who is to blame for the killings? The killers are to blame.

"Illegitimacy is something we should talk about in terms of not having it."

"We are ready for any unforeseen event that may or may not occur."

"For NASA, space is still a high priority."

"Quite frankly, teachers are the only profession that teach our children."

"The American people would not want to know of any misquotes that Al Gore may or may not make."

"We're all capable of mistakes, but I do not care to enlighten you on the mistakes we may or may not have made."

"It isn't pollution that's harming the environment. It's the impurities in our air and water that are doing it."

"[It's] time for the human race to enter the solar system."

NOTICE OF REVOCATION OF INDEPENDENCE

To the citizens of the United States of America,
In the light of your failure to elect a President of the USA and thus to govern yourselves, we hereby give notice of the revocation of your independence, effective today.
Her Sovereign Majesty Queen Elizabeth II will resume monarchial duties over all states, commonwealths and other territories. Except Utah, which she does not fancy. Your new prime minister (The rt. hon. Tony Blair, MP for the 97.85% of you who have until now been unaware that there is a world outside your borders) will appoint a minister for America without the need for further elections.
Congress and the Senate will be disbanded. A questionnaire will be circulated next year to determine whether any of you noticed.
To aid in the transition to a British Crown Dependency, the following rules are introduced with immediate effect:
1. You should look up "revocation" in the Oxford English Dictionary. Then look up "aluminium". Check the pronunciation guide. You will be amazed at just how wrongly you have been pronouncing it. Generally, you should raise your vocabulary to acceptable levels. Look up "vocabulary". Using the same twenty seven words interspersed with filler noises such as "like" and "you know" is an unacceptable and inefficient form of communication. Look up "interspersed".
2. There is no such thing as "US English". We will let Microsoft know on your behalf.
3. You should learn to distinguish the English and Australian accents. It really isn't that hard.
4. Hollywood will be required occasionally to cast English actors as the good guys.
5. You should relearn your original national anthem, "God Save The Queen", but only after fully carrying out task 1. We would not want you to get confused and give up half way through.
6. You should stop playing American "football". There is only one kind of football. What you refer to as American "football" is not a very good game. The 2.15% of you who are aware that there is a world outside your borders may have noticed that no one else plays "American" football. You will no longer be allowed to play it, and should instead play proper football. Initially, it would be best if you played with the girls. It is a difficult game. Those of you brave enough will, in time, be allowed to play rugby (which is similar to American "football", but does not involve stopping for a rest every twenty seconds or wearing full kevlar body armour like nancies). We are hoping to get together at least a US rugby sevens side by 2010.

7. You should declare war on Quebec and France, using nuclear weapons if they give you any merde. The 98.85% of you who were not aware that there is a world outside your borders should count yourselves lucky. The Russians have never been the bad guys. "Merde" is French for "shit".
8. July 4th is no longer a public holiday. November 8th will be a new national holiday, but only in England. It will be called "Indecisive Day".
9. All American cars are hereby banned. They are crap and it is for your own good. When we show you German cars, you will understand what we mean.
10. Please tell us who killed JFK. It's been driving us crazy.

Thank you for your cooperation.

Stanley Cup

It's Game 7 of the Stanley Cup Final, and a man makes his way to his seat right at center ice.
He sits down, noticing that the seat next to him is empty.
He leans over and asks his neighbor if someone will be sitting there. "No," says the neighbor. "The seat is empty."
"This is incredible", said the man.
"Who in their right mind would have a seat like this for final game of the Stanley Cup playoffs and not use it?"
The neighbour "Well, actually, the seat belongs to me.
I was supposed to come with my wife, but she passed away.
This is the first Stanley Cup we haven't been to together since we got married in 67."
"Oh ... I'm sorry to hear that. That's terrible. But couldn't you find someone else, a friend or relative, or even a neighbor to take the seat?"
The man shakes his head:
"No. They're all at the funeral."

Studying

Boy to mother: I've decided to stop studying.'
'How come?' asked the mother.
'I heard that someone was shot dead, because he knew too much.'

Who to Marry and Why
(As answered by elementary school students)

HOW DO YOU DECIDE WHO TO MARRY?

You got to find somebody who likes the same stuff.
Like, if you like sports, she should like it that you like sports, and she should keep the chips and dip coming.
Alan, age 10

No person really decides before they grow up who they're going to marry. God decides it all way before, and you get to find out later who you're stuck with.
Kirsten, age 10

WHAT IS THE RIGHT AGE TO GET MARRIED?
Twenty-three is the best age because you know the person FOREVER by then.
Camille, age 10

No age is good to get married at. You got to be a fool to get married.
Freddie, age 6

HOW CAN A STRANGER TELL IF TWO PEOPLE ARE MARRIED?
You might have to guess, based on whether they seem to be yelling at the same kids.
Derrick, age 8

WHAT DO YOU THINK YOUR MOM AND DAD HAVE IN COMMON?
Both don't want any more kids.
Lori, age 8

WHAT DO MOST PEOPLE DO ON A DATE?
Dates are for having fun, and people should use them to get to know each other. Even boys have something to say if you listen long enough.
Lynnette, age 8

On the first date, they just tell each other lies, and that usually gets them interested enough to go for a second date.
Martin, age 10

WHAT WOULD YOU DO ON A FIRST DATE THAT WAS TURNING SOUR?
I'd run home and play dead. The next day I would call all the newspapers and make sure they wrote about me in all the dead columns.
Craig, age 9

WHEN IS IT OKAY TO KISS SOMEONE?
When they're rich.
Pam, age 7

The law says you have to be eighteen, so I wouldn't want to mess with that.
Curt, age 7

The rule goes like this: If you kiss someone, then you should marry them and have kids with them. It's the right thing to do.
Howard, age 8

IS IT BETTER TO BE SINGLE OR MARRIED?
It's better for girls to be single but not for boys.
Boys need someone to clean up after them.
Anita, age 9

HOW WOULD THE WORLD BE DIFFERENT IF PEOPLE DIDN'T GET MARRIED?
There sure would be a lot of kids to explain, wouldn't there?
Kelvin, age 8

HOW WOULD YOU MAKE A MARRIAGE WORK?
Tell your wife that she looks pretty even if she looks like a truck.
Ricky, age 10

Sentencing

A judge looked severely at the defendant and asked, 'How many times have you been imprisoned?'
'Nine, your Honour.'
'Nine? In this case, I will give you the maximum sentence.'
'Maximum sentence?' said the defendant. 'Don't you give your regular clients a discount?'

Not too smart!

I am a medical student currently doing a rotation in toxicology at the poison control center. Today, this woman called in very upset because she caught her little daughter eating ants. I quickly reassured her that the ants are not harmful and there would be no need to bring her daughter into the hospital. She calmed down, and at the end of the conversation happened to mention that she gave her daughter some ant poison to eat in order to kill the ants. I told her that she better bring her daughter into the Emergency Room right away.

Seems that a year ago, some Boeing employees on the airfield decided to steal a life raft from one of the 747s. They were successful in getting it out of the plane and home. When they took it for a float on the river, they were surprised by a Coast Guard helicopter coming towards them. It turned out that the chopper was homing in on the emergency locator that is activated when the raft is inflated. They are no longer employed at Boeing.

A guy walked into a little corner store with a shotgun and demanded all the cash from the cash drawer. After the cashier put the cash in a bag, the robber saw a bottle of scotch that he wanted behind the counter on the shelf. He told the cashier to put it in the bag as well, but he refused and said, "Because I don't believe you are over 21." The robber said he was, but the clerk still refused to give it to him because he didn't believe him. At this point the robber took his driver's license out of his wallet and gave it to the clerk. The clerk looked it over, and agreed that the man was in fact over 21 and he put the scotch in the bag. The robber then ran from the store with his loot. The cashier promptly called the police and gave the name and address of the robber that he got off the license. They arrested the robber two hours later.

A pair of Michigan robbers entered a record shop, nervously waving revolvers. The first one shouted, "Nobody move!" When his partner moved, the startled first bandit shot him.

Arkansas: Seems this guy wanted some beer pretty badly. He decided that he'd just throw a cinder block through a liquor store window, grab some booze, and run. So he lifted the cinder block and heaved it over his head at the window. The cinder block bounced back and hit the would-be thief on the head, knocking him unconscious. Seems the liquor store window was made of Plexiglas. The whole event was caught on videotape.

Ann Arbor: The Ann Arbor News crime column reported that a man walked into a Burger King in Ypsilanti, Michigan at 12:50am, flashed a gun and demanded cash. The clerk turned him down because he said he couldn't open the cash register without a food order. When the man ordered onion rings, the clerk said they weren't available for breakfast. The man, frustrated, walked away.

A true story out of San Francisco: A man, wanting to rob a downtown Bank of America, walked into the branch and wrote "This iz a stikkup. Put all your muny in this bag." While standing in line, waiting to give his note to the teller, he began to worry that someone had seen him write the note and might call the police before he reached the teller window. So he left the Bank of America and crossed the street to Wells Fargo. After waiting a few minutes in line, he handed his note to the Wells Fargo teller. She read it and, surmising from his spelling errors that he wasn't the brightest light in the harbor, told him that she could not accept his stickup note because it was written on a Bank of America deposit slip and that he would either have to fill out a Wells Fargo deposit slip or go back to Bank of America. Looking somewhat defeated, the man said "OK" and left. He was arrested few minutes later, as he was waiting in line back at Bank of America.

A motorist was unknowingly caught in an automated speed trap that measured his speed using radar and photographed his car. He later received in the mail a ticket for $40 and a photo of his car. Instead of payment, he sent the police department a photograph of $40. Several days later, he received a letter from the police that contained another picture of handcuffs.

Preferences

After a two-year long study, the National Science Foundation announced the following results on corporate America's recreation preferences:
1. The sport of choice for unemployed or incarcerated people is: Basketball.
2. The sport of choice for maintenance level employees is: Bowling.
3. The sport of choice for front line workers is: Football.
4. The sport of choice for supervisors is: Baseball.
5. The sport of choice for middle management is: Tennis.
6. The sport of choice for corporate officers is: Golf.
Conclusion:
The higher you are in the corporate structure, the smaller your balls become.

Pregnancy

Q: Should I have a baby after 35?
A: No, 35 children is enough.

Q: I'm two months pregnant now. When will my baby move?
A: With any luck, right after he finishes college.

Q: How will I know if my vomiting is morning sickness or the flu?
A: If it's the flu, you'll get better.

Q: Since I became pregnant, my breasts, rear end, and even my feet have grown.
Is there anything that gets smaller during pregnancy?
A: Yes, your bladder.

Q: What is the most common pregnancy craving?
A: For men to be the ones who get pregnant.

Q: What is the most reliable method to determine a baby's sex?
A: Childbirth.

Q: The more pregnant I get, the more often strangers smile at me. Why?
A: 'Cause you're fatter than they are.

Q: My wife is 5 months pregnant, so moody sometimes she's borderline irrational.
A: So what's your question?

Q: What's the difference between a nine-month pregnant woman and a model?
A: Nothing, if the pregnant woman's husband knows what's good for him.

Q: How long is the average woman in labor?
A: Whatever she says divided by two.

Q: My childbirth instructor says it's not pain I'll feel during labor, but pressure. Is
she right?
A: Yes, in the same way that a tornado might be called an air current.

Q: When is the best time to get an epidural?
A: Right after you find out you're pregnant.

Q: Is there any reason I have to be in the delivery room while my wife is in labor?
A: Not unless the word "alimony" means anything to you.

Q: What does it mean when the baby's head is crowning?
A: It means you feel as though not only a crown but the entire throne is trying to make its way out of you.

Q: Is there anything I should avoid while recovering from childbirth?
A: Yes, pregnancy.

Q: Does pregnancy cause hemorrhoids?
A: Pregnancy causes anything you want to blame it for.

Q: Where is the best place to store breast milk?
A: In your breasts.

Q: Is there a safe alternative to breast pumps?
A: Yes, baby lips.

Q: What does it mean when a baby is born with teeth?
A: It means that the baby's mother may want to rethink her plans to nurse.

Q: How does one sanitize nipples?
A: Bathe daily and wear a clean bra. It beats boiling them in a saucepan.

Q: What are the terrible twos?
A: Your breasts after baby stops nursing cold turkey.

Q: What is the best time to wean the baby from nursing?
A: When you see teeth marks.

Q: Do I have to have a baby shower?
A: Not if you change the baby's diaper very quickly.

Q: Our baby was born last week. When will my wife begin to feel and act normal again?
A: When the kids are in college.

Pain

A young brunette goes into the doctor's office and tells him that her body hurts wherever she touches it.

"Impossible," says the doctor. "Show me."

She takes her finger and pushes on her elbow and screams in agony.

She then pushes on her knee and screams, pushes on her ankle and screams...and so it goes.

No matter where she touches her agony is apparent.

The doctor says, "You're not really a brunette, are you? You're really a blonde."

She sheepishly admits that indeed she is a blonde.

"I thought so," he says.

"Your finger is broken."

Mental

Jim and Mary were both patients in a Mental Hospital. One day while they were walking past the hospital swimming pool, Jim suddenly jumped into the deep end. He sunk to the bottom and stayed there. Mary promptly jumped in to save him. She swam to the bottom and pulled Jim out.

When the medical director became aware of Mary's heroic act he immediately ordered her to be discharged from the hospital, as he now considered her to be mentally stable.

When he went to tell Mary the news he said, "Mary, I have good news and bad news. The good news is you're being discharged because since you were able to jump in and save the life of another patient, I think you've regained your senses. The bad news is, Jim, the patient you saved, hung himself with his bathrobe belt in the bathroom. I am so sorry, but he's dead."

Mary replied "He didn't hang himself, I put him there to dry."

Sugar

Staying at a small-town hotel, Tom ordered tea. Shortly afterwards, a girl threw open the door. 'Sugar in your tea?' she shouted.

'No, thank you,' Tom replied.

'Ah, well, don't stir it then.'

Two Cows

Political and Corporate Philosophies Explained in Simple Two Cow Terms.

SOCIALISM
You have two cows. You keep one and give one to your neighbor.

COMMUNISM
You have two cows, the government takes them both and provides you with milk.

FASCISM
You have two cows, the government takes them and sells you the milk.

BUREAUCRACY
You have two cows. The government takes them both, shoots one, milks the other, pays you for the milk, and then pours it down the drain.

DEMOCRACY
You have two cows, the government taxes you to the point that you must sell them both in order to support a man in a foreign country that has only one cow which was a gift from your government.

TRADITIONAL CAPITALISM
You have two cows.
You sell one and buy a bull.
Your herd multiplies, and the economy grows.
You sell the herd and retire on the income.

AN AMERICAN CORPORATION
You have two cows.
You sell one, and force the other to produce the milk of four cows.
You are surprised when the cow drops dead.

A FRENCH CORPORATION
You have two cows.
You go on strike because you want three cows.

A JAPANESE CORPORATION
You have two cows.
You re-design them so they are one-tenth the size of an ordinary cow and produce twenty times the milk. You then create irritating cow cartoon images called Cowkimon and market them world-wide at a fantastic profit.

A GERMAN CORPORATION
You have two cows.
You re-engineer them so they live for 100 years, eat once a month, and milk themselves.

AN ENGLISH CORPORATION
You have two cows.
Both are mad.

AN ITALIAN CORPORATION
You have two cows, but you don't know where they are.
You break for lunch.

A RUSSIAN CORPORATION
You have two cows.
You count them and learn you have five cows.
You count them again and learn you have 42 cows.
You count them again and learn you have 12 cows.
You stop counting cows and open another bottle of vodka.

A SWISS CORPORATION
You have 5000 cows, none of which belong to you.
You charge others for storing them.

A HINDU CORPORATION
You have two cows.
You worship them.

A CHINESE CORPORATION
You have two cows.
You have 300 people milking them.
You claim full employment, high bovine productivity, and arrest the newsman who reported the numbers.

A WELSH CORPORATION
You have two cows.
The younger one is rather attractive.

AN AUSTRALIAN CORPORATION
Western suburbs style....
You have 2 stolen bulls but think they are cows.
You die the first time you try and milk them.

AN IRISH CORPORATION
Who cares, the EU really owns them now and the pub is still serving.

A NEW ZEALAND CORPORATION
You have two cows.
You don't know what they are used for as they aren't sheep. You **** them anyway.

Shamus Mahoney

Brenda Mahoney is making dinner when Tim Finnegan arrives at her door.
"Brenda, may I come in?" he asks, "I've got something to tell you."
"Of course," she answers. "You're always welcome, Tim. But where's my husband?"
"That's what I'm here to be telling ya, Brenda. There was an accident at the brewery."
"Oh God, no . . " cries Brenda. "Please don't' tell me . ."
"I must Brenda. Your husband, Shamus, is dead and gone. I'm sorry."
After a long pause, Brenda looks up an asks, "How did it happen, Tim?"
"It was terrible, Brenda. He fell into a vat of Guinness Stout and drowned."
"Oh my dear Jesus! But tell me, did he go quickly?"
"Well no Brenda . . . no."
"No?"
"Fact is, he got out three times to pee."

What do women really want?

Young King Arthur was ambushed and imprisoned by the monarch of a
neighboring kingdom. The monarch could have killed him, but was moved by
Arthur's youth and ideals. So the monarch offered him freedom, as long as he
could answer a very difficult question. Arthur would have a year to figure out the
answer; if, after a year, he still had no answer, he would be put to death.
The question: What do women really want?
Such a question would perplex even the most knowledgeable man, and, to young
Arthur, it seemed an impossible query. But, since it was better than death, he
accepted the monarch's proposition to have an answer by year's end. He returned to
his kingdom and began to poll everybody: the princess, the prostitutes, the priests,
the wise men, the court jester. He spoke with everyone, but no one could give him
a satisfactory answer. Many people advised him to consult the old witch--only she
would know the answer.
The price would be high; the witch was famous throughout the kingdom for the
exorbitant prices she charged. The last day of the year arrived and Arthur had no
alternative but to talk to the witch.
She agreed to answer his question, but he'd have to accept her price first:
The old witch wanted to marry Gawain, the most noble of the Knights of the
Round Table and Arthur's closest friend! Young Arthur was horrified: She was
hunchbacked and hideous, had only one tooth, smelled like sewage, made obscene
noises... etc. He had never encountered such a repugnant creature.
He refused to force his friend to marry her and have to endure such a burden.
Gawain, upon learning of the proposal, spoke with Arthur. He told him that
nothing was too big a sacrifice compared to Arthur's life and the preservation of
the Round Table. Hence, their wedding was proclaimed, and the witch answered
Arthur's question thus:
What a woman really wants is to be in charge of her own life.
Everyone instantly knew that the witch had uttered a great truth and that Arthur's
life would be spared. And so it was. The neighboring monarch granted Arthur total
freedom. What a wedding Gawain and the witch had! Arthur was torn between
relief and anguish. Gawain was proper as always, gentle and courteous. The old
witch put her worst manners on display, and generally made everyone very
uncomfortable. The hour approached. Gawain, steeling himself for a horrific
experience, entered the bedroom. But what a sight awaited him!
The most beautiful woman he'd ever seen lay before him! The astounded Gawain
asked what had happened. The beauty replied that since he had been so kind to her
when she'd appeared as a witch, she would henceforth be her horrible, deformed

self half the time, and the other half, she would be her beautiful maiden self. Which would he want her to be during the day, and which during the night? What a cruel question! Gawain pondered his predicament.

During the day, a beautiful woman to show off to his friends, but at night, in the privacy of his home, an old witch? Or would he prefer having by day a hideous witch, but by night a beautiful woman with whom to enjoy many intimate moments?

What would you do? What Gawain chose follows below, but don't read until you've made your own choice.

Have you made your choice?????

Noble Gawain replied that he would let her choose for herself. Upon hearing this, she announced that she would be beautiful all the time, because he had respected her enough to let her be in charge of her own life.

What is the moral of this story?

The moral is: if your woman doesn't get her own way, things are going to get ugly!

Lunch in Wales

Two tourists were driving through Wales. As they were approaching Llanfairpwllgwyngyllgogerychwyrndrobwllllantysiliogogogoch they started arguing about the pronunciation of the town's name. They argued back and forth until they stopped for lunch. As they stood at the counter, one tourist asked the blonde employee, "Before we order, could you please settle an argument for us? Would you please pronounce where we are... very slowly?"

The girl leaned over the counter and said, "Burrrrrrrr, gerrrrrrr, Kiiiiing."

Violin

Little Johnny was practicing the violin in the living room, while his father was trying to read. The family dog was there, too, and, on hearing the screeching sounds, began to howl. Johnny's father listened to the dog and the violin for as long as he could. Then he jumped up, slammed his newspaper on the floor and yelled, 'For God's sake, can't you play something the dog doesn't know?'

Mothers

A young man excitedly tells his mother he's fallen in love and is going to get married.
He says, "Just for fun, Ma, I'm going to bring over 2 other female friends in addition to my fiancee and you try and guess which one I'm going to marry."
The next day, he brings 3 beautiful women into the house and sits them down on the couch and they chat for a while.
He then says, "Okay, Ma. Guess which one I'm going to marry."
She immediately replies, "The red-head in the middle."
"That's amazing, Ma. You're right, how did you know?"
"I don't like her."

Beers

A man walks into a bar and asks for a beer. After drinking it, he looks in his shirt pocket and asks for another beer.
After drinking that one, he looks in his shirt pocket again and asks for another beer. This happens about another seven times before the bartender asks him,
"Why do you keep looking in your pocket?"
The man replies, "I have a picture of my wife in there. When she looks good enough, I'll go home."

Flies

A woman walked into the kitchen to find her husband stalking around with a fly-swatter.
"What are you doing?" She asked.
"Hunting Flies"
"Oh!, have you got any?" She asked.
"Yep, 3 males, 2 females", he replied.
Intrigued, she asked. "How can you tell?"
"Well, 3 were on a beer can and 2 were on the phone".

Words Women Use

FINE
This is the word we use at the end of any argument that we feel we are right about but need to shut you up. NEVER use fine to describe how a woman looks. This will cause you to have one of those arguments.

FIVE MINUTES
This is half an hour. It is equivalent to the five minutes that your football game is going to last before you take out the trash, so that it's an even trade.

NOTHING
This means something and you should be on your toes. "Nothing" is usually used to describe the feeling a woman has of wanting to turn you inside out, upside down, and backwards. "Nothing" usually signifies an argument that will last "Five Minutes" and end with the word "Fine."

GO AHEAD (with raised eyebrows)
This is a dare. One that will result in a woman getting upset over "Nothing" and will end with the word "Fine."

GO AHEAD (normal eyebrows)
This means "I give up" or "Do what you want because I don't care."
You will get a raised eyebrow "Go Ahead" in just a few minutes, followed by "Nothing" and "Fine" and she will talk to you in about "Five Minutes" when she cools off.

LOUD SIGH
This is not actually a word, but is still often a verbal statement very misunderstood by men. A "Loud Sigh" means she thinks you are an idiot at that moment and wonders why she is wasting her time standing here and arguing with you over "Nothing."

SOFT SIGH
Again, not a word, but a verbal statement. "Soft Sighs" are one of the few things that some men actually understand. She is content. Your best bet is to not move or breathe and she will stay content.

THAT'S OKAY
This is one of the most dangerous statements that a woman can say to a man.
"That's Okay" means that she wants to think long and hard before paying you
retributions for whatever it is that you have done. "That's Okay" is often used with
the word "Fine" and used in conjunction with a raised eyebrow "Go Ahead." At
some point in the near future when she has plotted and planned, you are going to
be in some mighty big trouble.

PLEASE DO
This is not a statement, it is an offer. A woman is giving you the chance to come
up with whatever excuse or reason you have for doing whatever it is that you have
done. You have a fair chance to tell the truth, so be careful and you shouldn't get a
"That's Okay."

THANKS
A woman is thanking you. Do not faint, just say you're welcome.

THANKS A LOT
This is much different than "Thanks." A woman will say, "Thanks A Lot" when
she is really ticked off at you. It signifies that you have hurt her in some callous
way, and will be followed by the "Loud Sigh." Be careful not to ask what is wrong
after the "Loud Sigh," as she will only tell you "Nothing."

Irishman

An Irishman who had a bit to drink is driving home weaving all over the road.
A cop pulls him over and asks, "So, where have you been?
"At the pub, of course," come the slurred answer.
"Well," says the cop, "looks like you had yourself quite a few pints."
"I did all right," says the drunk, grinning.
"Did you know," says the cop, "that a few blocks back your wife fell out of the
car?"
"Oh, thank goodness," sighs the drunk. "For a minute there I thought I'd gone
deaf."

Math

Little Tommy (who was Jewish) was doing very badly in math.
His parents had tried everything: tutors, they tried everything they could think of.
Finally, in a last ditch effort, they took Tommy down and enrolled him in the local Catholic school.
After the first day, little Tommy came home with a very serious look on his face.
He didn't even kiss his mother hello.
Instead, he went to his room and started studying.
Books and papers were spread out all over the room and little Tommy was at work. His mother was amazed.
She called him down to dinner and to her shock, the minute he was done he marched back to his room without a word and in no time he was back hitting the books as hard as before.
This went on for some time, day after day while the mother tried to understand what made all the difference.
Finally, little Tommy brought home his report card. He quietly laid it on the table and went up to his room and hit the books.
With great trepidation, his Mom looked at it and to her surprise, little Tommy got an A in math.
She could no longer hold her curiosity.
She went to his room and said:
"Son, what was it???? Was it the nuns??"
Little Tommy looked at her and shook his head, no.
"Well, then", she replied, "was it the books, the discipline, the structure, the uniforms???? WHHHHAAAATTTT was it????"
Little Tommy looked at her and said, "Well, on the first day of school, when I saw that guy nailed to the plus sign, I knew they weren't fooling around!"

Job interview

An eager young man entered his prospective boss' cabin for an interview. Said the boss: 'One thing our company is very particular about is cleanliness. I hope you wiped your shoes on the doormat while coming in?'
'Yes sir,' the young man replied promptly.
Back came the rejoinder: 'One more thing we're very particular about is honesty. There is no doormat outside!'

Men and Women

1. EATING OUT:
When the bill arrives, men will each throw in a $20, even though the bill is only for $22.50. None of them will have anything smaller, and no one will actually admit they want change back.
When the girls get their bill, out come the pocket calculators.

2. MONEY:
A man will pay $2 for a $1 item he really wants.
A woman will pay $1 for a $2 item that she doesn't really want.

3. BATHROOMS:
A man has five items in his bathroom: a toothbrush, shaving cream, razor, a bar of soap, and a towel from the Holiday Inn.
The average number of items in the typical woman's bathroom is 437. A man would not be able to identify most of these items, and would be afraid to REALLY know what they are for.

4. ARGUMENTS:
A woman has the last word in any argument.
Anything a man says after that is the beginning of a new argument.

5. FUTURE:
A woman worries about the future until she gets a husband.
A man never worries about the future until he gets a wife.

6. SUCCESS:
A successful man is one who makes more money than his wife can spend.
A successful woman is one who can find such a man.

7. MARRIAGE:
A woman marries a man expecting he will change, but he doesn't.
A man marries a woman expecting that she won't change and she does.

8. DRESSING UP:
A woman will dress up to: go shopping, water the plants, empty the garbage, answer the phone, read a book, get the mail.

A man will dress up for weddings and funerals.

9. HAPPINESS:
To be happy with a man, you must understand him a lot and love him a little.
To be happy with a woman, you must love her a lot and not try to understand her at all.

10. LONG LIFE:
Married men live longer than single men, but married men are a lot more willing to die.

11. MISTAKES:
Any married man should forget his mistakes.
There's no use in two people remembering the same thing.

12. NATURAL:
Men wake up as good-looking as they went to bed.
Women somehow deteriorate during the night.

13. OFFSPRING:
Ah, children. A woman knows all about her children. She knows about dentist appointments and romances, best friends, and favorite foods and secret fears and hopes and dreams.
A man is vaguely aware of some short people living in the house.

14. UNDERSTANDING:
There are two times when a man doesn't understand a woman, before marriage and after marriage.

Pay

The employee stormed angrily into the cashier's office. 'What's the meaning of this? I just counted my pay and it's a dollar short!'
The cashier examined the envelope, then checked his records. 'Last week we paid you a dollar more. You didn't complain then, did you?'
'Look' said the employee. 'An occasional mistake I can overlook – but two in a row is too much!'

Phrases

"When I die, I want to die like my grandfather, who died peacefully in his sleep. Not screaming like all the passengers in his car."
Author Unknown

Advice for the day: If you have a lot of tension and you get headache, do what it says on the aspirin bottle:
"Take two aspirin" and "Keep away from children"
Author Unknown

"Oh, you hate your job? Why didn't you say so? There's a support group for that. It's called EVERYBODY, and they meet at the bar."
Drew Carey

"Instead of getting married again, I'm going to find a woman I don't like and just give her a house."
Rod Stewart

"The problem with the designated driver program, it's not a desirable job, but if you ever get sucked into doing it, have fun with it. At the end of the night, drop them off at the wrong house."
Jeff Foxworthy

"If a woman has to choose between catching a fly ball and saving an infant's life, she will choose to save the infant's life without even considering if there is a man on base."
Dave Barry

"Relationships are hard. It's like a full time job, and we should treat it like one. If your boyfriend or girlfriend wants to leave you, they should give you two weeks' notice. There should be severance pay, and before they leave you, they should have to find you a temp."
Bob Ettinger

"My Mom said she learned how to swim when someone took her out in the lake and threw her off the boat. I said, 'Mom, they weren't trying to teach you how to swim.'"
Paula Poundstone

"A study in the Washington Post says that women have better verbal skills than men. I just want to say to the authors of that study: "Duh."
Conan O'Brien

"Why does Sea World have a seafood restaurant?? I'm halfway through my fish burger and I realize, Oh my God.... I could be eating a slow learner."
Lynda Montgomery

"This is how Chicago got started. A bunch of people in New York said, 'Gee, I'm enjoying the crime and the poverty, but it just isn't cold enough. Let's go west.'"
Richard Jeni

"If life were fair, Elvis would be alive and all the impersonators could be dead."
Johnny Carson

"Sometimes I think war is God's way of teaching us geography."
Paul Rodriguez

"My parents didn't want to move to Florida, but they turned sixty, and that's the law."
Jerry Seinfeld

"Remember in elementary school, you were told that in case of fire you have to line up quietly in a single file line from smallest to tallest. What is the logic in that? What, do tall people burn slower?"
Warren Hutcherson

"Our bombs are smarter than the average high school student. At least they can find Afghanistan."
A. Whitney Brown

"Women complain about premenstrual syndrome, but I think of it as the only time of the month that I can be myself."
Roseanne

"You can say any foolish thing to a dog, and the dog will give you a look that says, 'My God, you're right! I never would've thought of that!'"
Dave Barry

Australian Tourism Website Queries

Three Aussie tourism staff have been recently reprimanded for their responses to email tourist questions - wonder why?

Q: Does it ever get windy in Australia? I have never seen it rain on TV, so how do the plants grow? (UK)
A: We import all plants fully grown and then just sit around watching them die.

Q: Can you give me some information about hippo racing in Australia? (USA)
A: A-fri-ca is the big triangle shaped continent south of Europe. Aus-tra-lia is that big island in the middle of the pacific which does not... oh forget it. Sure, the hippo racing is every Tuesday night in Kings Cross. Come naked.

Q: Will I be able to speek (sic) English most places I go? (USA)
A: Yes, but you'll have to learn it first.

Q: Will I be able to see kangaroos in the street? (USA)
A: Depends how much you've been drinking.

Q: I want to walk from Perth to Sydney - can I follow the railroad tracks? (Sweden)
A: Sure, it's only three thousand miles, take lots of water...

Q: Is it safe to run around in the bushes in Australia? (Sweden)
A: So it's true what they say about Swedes.

Q: It is imperative that I find the names and addresses of places to contact for a stuffed porpoise. (Italy)
A: Let's not touch this one.

Q: Are there any ATMs (cash machines) in Australia? Can you send me a list of Brisbane, Cairns, Townsville and Hervey Bay? (UK)
A: Hey, what did your last slave die of?

Q: Which direction is North in Australia? (USA)
A: Face south and then turn 90 degrees. Contact us when you get here and we'll send the rest of the directions.

Q: Can I bring cutlery into Australia? (UK)
A: Why? Just use your fingers like we do.

Q: Can you send me the Vienna Boys' Choir schedule? (USA)
A: Aus-tri-a is that quaint little country bordering Ger-man-y, which is...oh forget it. Sure, the Vienna Boys Choir plays every Tuesday night in Kings Cross, straight after the hippo races. Come naked.

Q: Do you have perfume in Australia? (France)
A: No, WE don't stink.

Q: I have developed a new product that is the fountain of youth. Can you tell me where I can sell it in Australia? (USA)
A: Anywhere significant numbers of Americans gather.

Q: Can I wear high heels in Australia? (UK)
A: You are a British politician, right?

Q: Do you celebrate Christmas in Australia? (France)
A: Only at Christmas.

Q: Are there killer bees in Australia? (Germany)
A: Not yet, but for you, we'll import them.

Q: Are there supermarkets in Sydney and is milk available all year round? (Germany)
A: No, we are a peaceful civilisation of vegan hunter gatherers. Milk is illegal.

Q: Please send a list of all doctors in Australia who can dispense rattlesnake serum. (USA)
A: Rattlesnakes live in A-meri-ca which is where YOU come from. All Australian snakes, like taipans, blacks & adders, are perfectly harmless, can be safely handled and make good pets.

Q: I have a question about a famous animal in Australia, but I forget its name. It's a kind of bear and lives in trees.
A: It's called a Drop Bear, because they drop out of gum trees and scratch and bite anyone walking underneath them. You can scare them off by spraying yourself with human urine, purchased at the pharmacy, before you go out walking.

Fight

Into a Belfast pub comes Paddy Murphy, looking like he'd just been run over by a train. His arm is in a sling, his nose is broken, his face is cut and bruised and he's walking with a limp.
"What happened to you?" asks Sean, the bartender.
"Jamie O'Conner and me had a fight," says Paddy.
"That little shit, O'Conner," says Sean, "He couldn't do that to you, he must have had something in his hand."
"That he did," says Paddy, "a shovel is what he had, and a terrible lickin' he gave me with it."
"Well," says Sean, "you should have defended yourself, didn't you have something in your hand?"
"That I did," said Paddy..... "Mrs. O'Conner's breast, and a thing of beauty it was, but useless in a fight."

Last request

Mary Clancy goes up to Father O'Grady after his Sunday morning service, and she's in tears. He says, "So what's bothering you, Mary my dear?"
She says, "Oh, Father, I've got terrible news. My husband passed away last night."
The priest says, "Oh, Mary, that's terrible. Tell me, Mary, did he have any last requests?"
She says, "That he did, Father."
The priest says, "What did he ask, Mary? " She says, "He said, 'Please Mary, put down that damn gun...'"

Against your will?

When Sarah confessed that she'd committed adultery, the good father asked: "Was it against your will?"
"Oh no," Sarah confessed. "It was against the china closet and it would have tickled your heart to hear the dishes rattle!"

Why Men Are Just Happier People

1. Your last name stays put.
2. The garage is all yours.
3. Wedding plans take care of themselves.
4. Chocolate is just another snack.
5. You can be president.
6. You can never be pregnant.
7. You can wear a white T-shirt to a water park.
8. You can wear NO T-shirt to a water park.
9. Car mechanics tell you the truth.
10. The world is your urinal.
11. You never have to drive to another gas station restroom because this one is just too icky.
12. You don't have to stop and think of which way to turn a nut on a bolt.
13. Same work, more pay.
14. Wrinkles add character.
15. Wedding dress $5000, Tux rental $100.
16. People never stare at your chest when you're talking to them.
17. The occasional well-rendered belch is practically expected.
18. New shoes don't cut, blister, or mangle your feet.
19. One mood - all the time.
20. Phone conversations are over in 30 seconds flat.
21. You know stuff about tanks.
22. A five-day vacation requires only one suitcase.
23. You can open all your own jars.
24. You get extra credit for the slightest act of thoughtfulness.
25. If someone forgets to invite you, he or she can still be your friend.
26. Your underwear is $8.95 for a three-pack.
27. Three pairs of shoes are more than enough.
28. You almost never have strap problems in public.
29. You are unable to see wrinkles in your clothes.
30. Everything on your face stays its original color.
31. The same hairstyle lasts for years, maybe decades.
32. You only have to shave your face and neck.
33. You can play with toys all your life.
34. Your belly usually hides your big hips.
35. One wallet and one pair of shoes one color for all seasons.
36. You can wear shorts no matter how your legs look.

37. You can "do" your nails with a pocketknife.
38. You have freedom of choice concerning growing a mustache.
39. You can do Christmas shopping for 25 relatives on December 24 in 45 minutes.

No wonder men are happier.

Science/Medical report language

The following list of phrases and their definitions might help you understand the mysterious language of science and medicine. These special phrases are also applicable to anyone reading a Ph.D. dissertation or academic paper.

1. IT HAS LONG BEEN KNOWN...
I didn't look up the original reference.

2. A DEFINITE TREND IS EVIDENT...
These data are practically meaningless.

3. WHILE IT HAS NOT BEEN POSSIBLE TO PROVIDE DEFINITE ANSWERS TO THESE QUESTIONS...
An unsuccessful experiment, but I still hope to get it published.

4. THREE OF THE SAMPLES WERE CHOSEN FOR DETAILED STUDY...
The other results didn't make any sense.

5. TYPICAL RESULTS ARE SHOWN...
This is the prettiest graph.

6. THESE RESULTS WILL BE IN A SUBSEQUENT REPORT...
I might get around to this sometime, if pushed/funded.

7. IN MY EXPERIENCE... Once.
IN CASE AFTER CASE... Twice.
IN A SERIES OF CASES... Thrice.
IT IS BELIEVED THAT... I think.
IT IS GENERALLY BELIEVED THAT... A couple of others think so, too.

8. CORRECT WITHIN AN ORDER OF MAGNITUDE...
Wrong.

9. ACCORDING TO STATISTICAL ANALYSIS...
Rumor has it.

10. A statistically oriented PROJECTION OF THE SIGNIFICANCE OF THESE FINDINGS...
A wild guess.

11. A CAREFUL ANALYSIS OF OBTAINABLE DATA...
Three pages of notes were obliterated when I knocked over a glass of beer.

12. IT IS CLEAR THAT MUCH ADDITIONAL WORK WILL BE REQUIRED BEFORE A COMPLETE UNDERSTANDING OF THIS PHENOMENON OCCURS...
I don't understand it.

13. AFTER ADDITIONAL STUDY BY MY COLLEAGUES...
They don't understand it either.

14. THANKS ARE DUE TO JOE BLOTZ FOR ASSISTANCE WITH THE EXPERIMENT AND TO CINDY ADAMS FOR VALUABLE DISCUSSIONS...
Dr. Blotz did the work and Ms. Adams explained to me what it meant.

15. A HIGHLY SIGNIFICANT AREA FOR EXPLORATORY STUDY...
A totally useless topic selected by my committee.

16. IT IS HOPED THAT THIS STUDY WILL STIMULATE FURTHER INVESTIGATION IN THIS FIELD...
I quit.

Robbery?

Late one night, a mugger wearing a ski mask jumped into the path of a well-dressed man and stuck a gun in his ribs. 'Give me your money,' he demanded. Indignant, the affluent man replied, 'You can't do this – I'm a politician!' 'In that case,' replied the robber, 'give me my money!'

Ticket

Three lawyers and three engineers were traveling by train to a conference.
At the station, each lawyer bought a ticket whereas the engineers bought only one ticket between them.
'How are you going to travel on a single ticket?' asked a lawyer.
'Wait and watch,' answered one of the engineers.
When they boarded the train, the lawyers took their seats, but the three engineers crammed into a toilet and closed the door behind them. Shortly after the train started, the ticket collector arrived. He knocked on the toilet door and asked, 'Ticket please.' The door opened just a crack and a single arm emerged with a ticket in hand. The ticket collector took it and moved on. Seeing this, the lawyers decided to do the same thing on the return trip.
So when they got to the station, they bought only one ticket.
To their astonishment, the engineers didn't buy any.
'How are you going to travel without a ticket?' asked one of the perplexed lawyers.
'Wait and watch,' answered an engineer.
In the train, the three engineers crammed into a toilet and the three lawyers into another nearby. Soon after the train started, one of the engineers got out of the toilet and walked to the one where the lawyers were hiding.
He knocked on the door and said, 'Ticket, please.'

Professors

A patient complains to a famous psychologist: 'Professor, I've been having terrible obsessions for years, and no one has ever been able to help me.'
'Who's been treating you until now?'
'Dr. La Rathor.'
'I see. He's an idiot. I'm curious to know what he advised you to do.'
'To come and see you.'

Quarrel

Husband and wife were in the midst of a violent quarrel, and hubby was losing his temper. 'Be careful,' he said to his wife. 'You'll bring out the beast in me.'
'So what?' his wife shot back. 'Who's afraid of a mouse?'

Ran away

'I'm very sorry to learn that your wife ran away with your drive,' said the friend to the old man.
'Oh, don't worry, I can drive.'

Decision

One man to another. 'I want to marry a smart woman, a good woman; a woman who'll make me happy.'
'Make up your mind.'

Effectiveness

A rather inebriated fellow on a bus was tearing up a newspaper into tiny pieces and throwing them out the window.
'Excuse me,' said the woman sitting next to him. 'But, would you mind explaining why you're doing this?'
'It scares away the elephants,' replied the drunk.
'But I don't see any elephants around here,' said the woman.
'Effective, isn't it?' crowed the drunk.

Diapers

After they had brought their first baby home from the hospital, a young wife suggested to her husband that he try his hand at changing diapers, 'I'm busy,' he said. 'I'll do the next one.'
The next time the baby was wet, she asked if he was now ready to learn how to change diapers. He looked puzzled. 'Oh,' he replied finally. 'I didn't mean the next diaper. I meant the next baby!'

Time

Annoyed wife to husband: "Can't you say we've been married twenty-four years instead of "almost a quarter of a century"?

Dancing

A young soldier who was on a twenty four-hour pass went to a dance in town and there met an attractive young woman. As they danced, he kept making passes at her but without much result. Finally, he said, 'Look sweetheart, I really go for you in a big way. But I don't have much time. I have to be back in the morning. I'd sure like to speed things up between us.'
'But I am dancing as fast as I can,' she protested wide-eyed.

Anger and exasperation

Little Ernie was having a problem with his homework.
'Dad,' he asked, 'What is the difference between "anger" and "exasperation"?'
'Well, son,' said his father, 'I'll give you a practical demonstration.'
His father picked up the phone and dialed a number.
'Hello,' said Ernie's father. 'Is Melvin there?'
'There is no one called Melvin here!' the voice replied. 'Why don't you look up numbers before you dial them?'
'You see?' said Ernie's father. 'That man was not at all happy with our call. But watch this!'
He then dialed the number again, and says, 'Hello, is Melvin there?'
'Now look here!' the voice said angrily. 'I told you there is no Melvin here! You have got a lot of nerve calling again!'
'Did you hear that?' Ernie's father asked. 'That was "anger". Now, I will show you what "exasperation" is!'
He dialed once again. And on hearing the voice at the other end, Ernie's father said: 'Hello! This is Melvin. Have there been any calls for me?'

First human beings

Teacher: 'Who were the first human beings?'
Pupil: 'Adam and Eve.'
Teacher: 'And what nationality were they?'
Pupil: 'Indian, of course.'
Teacher: 'And how do you know they were Indian?'
Pupil: 'Easy. They had no roof over their heads, no clothes to wear and only one apple between them – and they called it Paradise.'

Marriage counselor

Husband to wife as they emerge from a long session with a marriage guidance counselor: 'Darling, I love you.'
'There you go again,' snapped his wife. 'I...I...I...again.'

Lawyer

The sign on the door of a lawyer's chamber reads: 'Where there is a will, there is a way; where there is a way, there is law; where there is law, there is a rule; where there is a rule, there is a loophole; where there is a loophole; there is a lawyer; and so here I am.'

Geography

Sonu was saying her bedtime prayers: 'Please God, make Naples the capital of Italy. Make Naples the capital of Italy,...'
'Why do you want God to make Naples the capital of Italy?' Sonu's mother asked.
And Sonu replied: 'Because, that is what I put in my Geography exam!'

Books

A teacher had just moved house with all her possessions including box after box of books.
As the van driver put down the last box in her second-floor flat, he grumbled, 'For Heaven's sake, lady, why didn't you read them before you came?'

Anesthetic

Doctor: 'Shall I give your wife a local anaesthetic?'
Businessman: 'Certainly not. I can afford something imported.'

Four jobs

Manager – 'From your references I see you've had four jobs in the last month.'
Applicant – 'Yes sir, but doesn't that show how much in demand I am?'

Husband

'How's your husband,?' Mrs. Mathur asked her friend.
'Pretty well, I think – he works so hard I see him for only about an hour each day.'
'You poor thing,' said Mrs. Mathur.
'Oh, its all right, the hour soon passes.'

Who shot Lincoln?

A not-too-bright candidate for the police force failed in the written examination.
Since he was the Chief's nephew, the examiner decided to go easy on him with the oral test.
'Who shot Abraham Lincoln?', asked the examiner.
The candidate pondered for a moment and then asked if he could have sometime to come up with the answer. The examiner told him to come back the next morning. When the would-be recruit went home, his wife asked, 'Well, how did it go? Did you get the job?'
'I think so,' he replied. 'They have already got me working on a case'.

Judge

Judge: 'The last time I saw you, I told you that I didn't want to see you here again.'
Accused: 'That is what I tried to tell these policemen, your Honour, but they would not believe me.'

Months

'What is your age?' asked the Judge. 'Remember you are under oath'.
'Twenty-one years and some months,' the woman answered.
'How many months?' the Judge persisted.
'One hundred and eight'.

Attention

He: 'I wonder why women pay more attention to beauty than to brains.'
She: 'Because no matter how stupid a man is, he is seldom blind.'

American vs Italian kids

American Kids: Move out when they're 18 with the full support of their parents.
Italian Kids: Move out when they're 28, having saved for that nice house and are a week away from getting married .... unless there's room in the basement for the newlyweds.

American Kids: When their Mom visits them she brings a nice bundt cake and you sip coffee and chat.
Italian Kids: When their Mom visits them she brings 3 days worth of food and begins to immediately tidy up, dust, do the laundry or rearrange the furniture.

American Kids: Their dads always call before they come over to visit them and its usually only on special occasions.
Italian Kids: Are not at all fazed when their dads come over, unannounced, on a Saturday morning at 8:00 and starts pruning the fruit trees. And if there are no fruit trees, he will plant some!

American Parents: You can leave your kids with them and you always worry if everything is going to be ok plus you have to feed them after you pick them up.
Italian Parents: No problem, leave your kids there and if they get out of line your parents can set them straight .... plus they get fed.

American Kids: Always pay retail and look in the yellow pages when they need something done.
Italian Kids: Just call their dad or uncle and ask for another dad's or uncle's phone number to get it done .... cash deal, knowwhatImean?

American Kids: Will come over for cake and coffee and get only cake and coffee, no more.
Italian Kids: Will come over for cake and coffee and get antipasto, a few bottles of wine, a pasta dish, a choice of two meats, salad, bread, potatoes, a nice dessert cake, fruit, coffee and a few after dinner drinks .... time permitting there will be a late lunch as well.

American Kids: Think that being Italian is a great thing.
Italian Kids: Know that being Italian is a great thing,

American Kids: Never ask the reason you have no food.
Italian Kids: Are the reason you have no food.

American Kids: Will say 'hello".
Italian Kids: Will give you a big hug and a kiss, pinch your cheeks, and pat you on the back.

American Kids: Call your parents Mr. and Mrs.
Italian Kids: Call your parents Mom and Dad.

American Kids: Have never seen you cry.
Italian Kids: Cry with you.

American Kids: Will eat at your dinner table and leave.
Italian Kids: Will spend hours there, talking, laughing and just being together.

American Kids: Borrow your stuff for a few days then give it back.
Italian Kids: Keep your stuff so long they forget it's yours.

American Kids: Know a few things about you.
Italian Kids: Could write a book with direct quotes from you.

American Kids: Will leave you behind if that's what the crowd is doing.
Italian Kids: Will kick the whole crowds' ass that left you.

American Kids: Would knock on your door.
Italian Kids: Walk right in and say, "I'm home!"

American Kids: Are for a while.
Italian Kids: Are for life.

American Kids: Will ignore this.
Italian Kids: Will forward this.

Dishonesty

Two employers were talking. Said one: 'I fear that young man I employed last week as a cashier is dishonest.'
'Oh,' replied the other, 'you shouldn't judge by appearances.'
'I'm not. I'm judging by disappearances!'

Formula

Chemistry Teacher: 'Can you give me the formula for water?'
Student: 'H-I-J-K-L-M-N-O'
Chemistry Teacher: 'Where did you get an idea like that?'
Student: 'You told us the other day it was H to O.'

Girls against marriage

He: 'There are an awful lot of girls who don't want to get married.'
She: 'How do you know?'
He: 'I've asked them.'

Fame

The aging actor was trying to chat up the gorgeous young girl.
'Don't you recognize me?' he asked. She shook her head.
'I'm quite well known in the movies,' he continued.
'Oh!' she said, her eyes lighting up. 'Where do you usually sit?'

Resemblance

The proud mother was showing off her new baby to her friend. 'Doesn't he look just like his father?' asked the mother.
'Yes,' replied the friend. 'But I shouldn't worry too much – he'll probably change for the better as he gets older.'

Promises

Pretty young girl: 'If I go up to your room do you promise to be good?'
Young man: 'Why – I promise to be FANTASTIC!'

Choosing books

Customer: 'I'd like to buy a novel, please.'
Bookshop assistant: 'Certainly, madam. Do you have the title or name of the author?'
Customer: 'Not really. I was hoping you could suggest something suitable.'
Bookshop assistant: 'No problem. Do you like light or heavy reading?'
Customer: 'It doesn't matter. I've left the car just outside the shop.'

Day off

Office worker: 'Sir?'
Boss: 'Yes? What is it now?'
Office worker: 'Please can I have a day off next week to do some late Christmas shopping with my wife and our six kids?'
Boss: 'Certainly not!'
Office worker: 'I knew you'd be understanding, sir. Thanks for getting me out of that terrible chore.'

Dictionary

Dogma: the mother of puppies.

Ultimate: the last person to marry.

Nurse

Pretty young nurse: 'Doctor, every time I take this young man's pulse it gets faster. Should I give him a sedative?'
Doctor: 'No. Just give him a blindfold.'

School

'Get up,' shouted Albert's mother. 'You'll be late for school.'

'But I don't want to go,' protested Albert. 'All the kids are horrible, the teachers are terrible, and it's all extremely boring. I want to stay home.'

'But,' replied Albert's mother, 'you're forty-three and the headmaster of the school.'

Cover and back cover by GJEMB